POLICE OFFICER

ALWAYS IN HARM'S WAY!

TOM K

THOMAS

The Empire Publishers publishing
12808 West Airport Blvd Suite 270M Sugar Land, TX 77478

https://empirepublishers.co/about-us

Our books may be purchased in bulk for promotional, educational, or business use.
Please contact The Empire Publishers at +(844) 636-4576, or by email at support@theempirepublishers.com

First Edition August 2024

Dedication

This book is dedicated to Jesus Christ, who is the only reason I am able to tell my stories in this book. All my life Jesus has protected me from all harm and death. He has guided me to work jobs and situations which made me successful in all my endeavors in life. Because of him I was able to perform well above my own abilities, for this and my salvation, I am humbly grateful. I will never understand his agape love for me and all of his followers.

About the Author

Tom K. Thomas is a retired police officer who has worked patrol, accident investigation, criminal investigation, juvenile bureau investigation and who taught the dare (drug abuse resistance education) program in the public schools.
His approach to being a police officer is that he always tried to help the people he came in contact with on a daily basis. Working in that manner many times got him into conflict with his superiors who cares mostly were about "making no waves."
Driven by a desire to help others, Tom often found himself advocating for those in need. This unwavering commitment sometimes placed him at further odds with superiors who prioritized a different approach. Even so, Tom never wavered in his belief that true law enforcement involves protecting and helping people, not just statistics.

Following his retirement, Tom translated his extensive experience into an impressive body of work. He served as a civil investigator for a major law firm, tackling complex cases ranging from auto accidents to medical malpractice.

Tom's impact extends far beyond casework. He actively shared his expertise by teaching numerous seminars and classes, including DWI detection, gang awareness, and horizontal gaze nystagmus, a technique for identifying impaired drivers.

Tom's dedication to learning is as impressive as his career. He holds a Bachelor's degree in Criminal Justice with a minor in Business Management, and has completed numerous classes, including those offered by the FBI and the National Highway Traffic Safety Administration.

Tom K. Thomas's story is one of unwavering dedication to justice and community. His experiences, both on the streets and in the classroom, paint a vivid picture of a man who has made a significant impact on the lives of countless individuals.

While these stories are based on actual events, names, locations and events have been changed and embellished. Any resemblance to people, locations and situations are purely coincidental.

Table of Contents

Chapter 1
The Man Inside

I was working robbery investigation with another team of detectives when I came across a very sad situation. We had a rash of robberies, about ten in that week, and all of these were being committed by the same guy. We had a lot of other robberies in general throughout the city at that time.

The other team got a break when a suspect's picture was picked out of a photo lineup by a robbery victim. We put out a "BOLO" (be on the lookout) on him and were watching a house where he was supposed to be frequenting. Our information on him included the fact that he had a $200-a-day drug habit. He started robbing people because his girlfriend, whom he was pimping to support his habit, could no longer work as a prostitute due to being sick and in the hospital.

While working on this case, one of the younger officers asked if we were going to have someone watch the hospital room where his girlfriend was, as the guy might try to see her. We all began to laugh because we knew that this habit he had would not let any feelings for anyone else stand in his way of taking care of himself and getting his drugs.

Feeding this habit was truly all he could think about. His girlfriend, a young and beautiful, or at least at one time slender lady, was dying. She was dying from "multiple incurable infections" which were the result of her using dirty needles. Probably the same needle that her boyfriend used himself. She was all alone in the hospital now. Who knows how she got started on drugs and prostitution. I am sure she did not expect this kind of end when she began her lifestyle. She died alone, quietly, I'm told.

It was very sad to me because I do remember her, some ten months earlier, calling officers names as they arrested her. She was very angry and independent at that time. In her opinion, we were all just giving her a "hard time." Why we couldn't just leave her alone, she kept screaming. It is sad; she deserved more out of life than what she got. I didn't know her, but I hurt inside thinking about her wasted life.

I feel sorry for this guy too. Oh, don't get me wrong, we arrested him and he will get about ten years for the robberies he committed. However, to be so messed up that all your waking moments are filled with thoughts of how to sell and use more drugs so you can "stop this 'man inside," as he put it, from hurting you is not on my list of favorites. He was so bad that when confronted by the arresting officers, he held a towel around his hand and pointed at the officers as if he had a gun.

When we asked him later why he did that, he said he wanted to "die easy" and that he was already dying hard and slow from the '"man inside."

Chapter 2
I Am Not Happy With My Life

"Car 4, 7819 Calumet, upstairs, rear. We got a report of an attempted suicide," the radio spluttered.

"Ten-four."

My partner and I were fairly close and arrived in less than a minute. The address was that of an apartment house in generally run-down condition. The front of the building was old brown brick, with some missing bricks and rotting wood trim in need of repair. The door was hanging half-open, and looking in and up, we could see a long, narrow stairway just inside. The steps were worn from use and dirty from neglect. I led the way up the steps with my partner Bill behind me.

A voice from behind us said, "You can't get in that way," in a half-crying tone.

"Did you call?" I asked as I turned and descended back down those creaky steps.

"Yeah, I called, but you can't get in that way because he's up against the door," he replied. "Come with me to the back door," he added, motioning for us to follow him.

We walked between this building and another to the south. I asked the man, "What's the problem?"

"Well, he's dead, you know?" he said as he stepped over old bottles, cans, and other items littering the tunnel.

"What is going on, man? Why would he do this?" the man asked.

"He left a note," he said."

"Who's hurt?" I replied.

"My brother hung himself, and he's still hanging; I couldn't get him down."

As he talked, our trio never even slowed down and finally exited the passageway between the buildings.

Once in the back, we walked to another set of stairs outside. As the man led us, we followed up these old, dirty white stairs. Our combined weight made the steps shift, creak, and groan as if they were objecting to the abuse we were putting on them. On the third landing, our watery-eyed leader pointed to a screen door and said, "He's in there."

As we walked into the room, straight across and up against the front door hung a youth about 17 years old. He was hanging from a brown belt which was digging into his neck. His tongue stuck out almost three inches, looking as if it was twice its normal size. It was so blue it almost looked black. His teeth, which once worked in perfect concert with his tongue, were now sunk into it as if his tongue was itself some tasty bit of food.

The young lad was hanging by the neck, eyes open and bulging as if they were peering into a darkened room. His knees were bent, and his feet were on the floor, stretched out in front of him as if he was leaning back into the door for support. His arms hung limp at his side: one fist clutched tight, the other open with his fingers stretched out as if reaching desperately for some unknown object. His hands seemed to show the extremes of two mechanical ends, one closed tight, and the other opened wide. I touched his face, and it felt as cold as a "dead fish." When I moved his arm, it was stiff and refused to move more than an inch, after which his entire body pivoted on the belt around his neck.

Other officers arrived as I stepped back from the hanging youth. They came to the front door and started pushing on the door, which held the lad, causing his arm to move along with his body. It was at this time that my partner walked back into the room.

"Don't move, you'll be okay," he said, thinking this kid was still alive and moving on his own.

"Bill," I said in a low voice, as his brother and other family members were on the porch, "he's not going to be okay, he's dead."

"Oh shit!" he exclaimed. Bill was kind of new, and I was breaking him in.

"Call and find out where the ambulance is, make sure they're coming," I said.

"But why?" he asked after he made the call and found out that they were almost on the scene. "You always call the paramedics no matter how obvious it is that he's dead," I replied. "Never take a chance on being wrong about something this serious."

The ambulance paramedic came in, pulled on the youth's arm, and smiled as he said, "You know he's dead, right?"

We shook our heads, and they began checking for vitals and getting the kid's name, leaving the lad hanging on the door like a trophy from a hunt.

The sergeant arrived, as did the crime lab, who took pictures of the kid, his room–which was dirty and cluttered with his possessions–and the note that he wrote, which bothered me. It was written with a very shaky hand and said, "I'm not happy with my life. I can't be happy no matter what I do. My stomach hurts from something I drank yesterday. I thought it would kill me then, but it just hurts. I was..." He didn't finish it. He "finished" himself instead.

During the autopsy, they found that he drank something the day before. They told us the chemical term for it, and I could have found out exactly what it was and where it came from, but what's the difference?

Before we left the scene, we helped the funeral home employee remove the boy from the room. Two of us held his arms, another held the belt just above his head, while he straddled the lifeless form, and still another forced the door open and removed the belt from its wedged position on top of the door against the jamb.

After laying him flat on the floor, we stood back as the funeral home guy stood on the stiff knees of the lad, forcing them down. As he did this, he looked at us with eager anticipation, expecting to see us squirm and thereby get some enjoyment. But he wasn't dealing with rookies, as the sergeant and I were the only two in the room at that time.

Sadly, the sergeant and I had seen worse things, so we just looked back as if to tell him to stop messing around and get the show on the road. This "ghoul" from the funeral home wanted our help. I slipped a "body bag" over the kid's feet, and pulled it up his legs, body, and over his head. The funeral home employee zipped it closed, and we lifted it onto his cart.

He left with the body and my partner got more facts from the family, such as date of birth, full name, and so on, for the report.

I stood alone in this room and thought about what must have gone through this kid's mind. How inventive he was to plan his demise in this fashion. The ceiling was too low for him to hang from it. Also, I wondered what he was about to say at the end of his note. Was it to his mom, dad, girlfriend, or to the world in general?

It seems to me that "last words," no matter how well articulated or "how illiterate" they are, should be written down somewhere for anybody to read if they want to.

For some time after that, we got the usual calls from the family wanting to know things like: Was he alive when we got there? Did he suffer? Even though the other son was there first, people always want answers from the uniformed police officer first on the scene. They also either ask you why he did it or if you have a lot of people do this sort of thing. You never really know what to say, and depending on the person, you try to tell them what they want or need to hear. Hopefully, you will find the words or something that will give them a little peace.

As always, no matter how much you were affected by this incident, you must bury those feelings and move on to the next call.

Chapter 3
½ Hours of a Working Day

I'm walking over railroad tracks, and it seems like there are a hundred of them. As I step between the rails of each track I go over, I occasionally step on a board between them, a railroad tie, my footing slips a little on the grease and oil that has fallen onto the board. It's a hot and humid night, and it's dark as hell in the switching yard. We got a call that someone was hurt in this switching yard. When I arrived, I was met by a railroad employee, a great big guy with one of those "football" type necks, a red face, a real "macho" type guy. Not in attitude, but in appearance, he was a masculine type of person. Anyway, he was leading me over these rails to where the accident occurred. I didn't know if the guy was dead at the time or not; all I knew was that there was an ambulance on the way and they sent me ahead to make sure everything was okay. If someone was dead, I had to secure the scene, make sure there was no "foul play," and if he wasn't dead, to see what I could do to help him until the ambulance arrived with paramedics.

As I walked over these tracks, making our way on a diagonal path from where I entered through a six-foot double gate, this guy didn't say much. He just kept walking a little bit in front of me and to my left. He had bib overalls on, and as we walked, every once in a while, he would rub his face, removing tears from his cheek. I started to get an uneasy feeling in my stomach the further we went. I didn't know what I was going to see, but I did know one thing–I didn't like situations like this. Give me some guy shooting at me before I have to go and see people die. That just screws me up; I can't handle that very well.

As we approached some boxcars, they were all dark. I couldn't tell if they were brown, gray, or what color. We started to walk to our right down the track that had boxcars parked to our right on it. Everything was quiet in the switching yard, which seemed unusual. I had driven by there many times and always noticed activity inside the yard. Cars switching and moving around, trains pulling cars to and fro, and people bustling about, creating what seemed like mass confusion. Most of the time, though, people never got hurt. I guess that was going to be different today.

As we walked down this aisle between two tracks bordered on our left now by this row of boxcars, I could see a lit area about a hundred feet in front of me. Someone put floodlights facing the boxcars. Between those lights and me, I could see a group of people standing outside. A group of men were milling around as if they were waiting for something to happen. Beyond them, I could see another group of people, a smaller group, that were also moving around in a nervous manner. I could see two or three people standing in between the cars. I still didn't know what had happened. I thought maybe someone got run over and dragged down the tracks, and they were looking at the body there.

I got a little bit closer, and I could now hear yells coming from the general area.

"Oh God, it hurts!"

“Someone help me, stop the pain! Damn, oh shit.”

"John, don't open it up! Don't open it up, John!" the cries came out.

I had this terrible feeling again. I knew by the sound of the voice and now the look on his face that he was dying. For some reason, I could look at someone's face and "read" their emotions. I could tell if they felt anger, fear, pain, or sorrow. I just knew, and it was easier than reading a book. I did that for seventeen years or more, and I'm good at it.

When I got a little bit closer yet, I could see more in between the cars, and there was a guy hanging there by his upper legs and his waist. Part of his belly was torn into by the train car coupling as he was coupled between two cars.

Oh crap, I remember this. It was something I could never figure out, but I knew it happened. I've been on two other ones, never this close and never by myself, though. You see, what happens is every once in a while, a worker switching cars will make a mistake, become a little careless, and get caught between two cars. They couple together as though he wasn't even there. He is just too close. He gets caught between the two couplings and it happens every time. Generally, he doesn't die right away. He'll hang there, linger on, suffer, and will live for, I don't know, maybe hours. The last one I was on sure seemed like hours to me. As long as they don't uncouple the cars, he'll remain squashed and hanging in that position. As soon as they open the cars, however, he'll fall over dead, as though someone threw a switch and turned his life off.

The doctor, a bald, heavy-set gentleman in his late fifties, was on the scene trying to keep his pain under control.

The company calls the doctor right away when it happens. It is one of the craziest things I ever heard of. They call the wife and kids too, so he can say goodbye to the dying person.

You see, he's hanging there, he's talking, this guy's even starting to light up a cigarette, but he's dead! All they're waiting for is for him to say goodbye to everyone. Then they're going to uncouple him and the cars, at which time he's going to die! They set this up with the switchman, other employees, management of the railroad, and the families; they all agree, that this is the way they want it to be handled. It's understood; everyone there, including me now, knew that he was dead! He was a talking dead man, just waiting to hit the ground. The doctor was giving him shots; I don't remember where. I wasn't looking that closely. I do remember his legs kind of pulled to the east of where the cars were. The train must have dragged him a while. His legs weren't moving; hell, they were hanging there like they were already dead. They probably were; it was just his brain that wasn't gone yet.

The coroner explained to me one time that what actually was happening was that everything in his body was crushed so badly that when you released the pressure caused by the coupling, which was holding all the crushed parts together, the hemorrhaging is so vast that there is nothing they can do to stop it, and the person just falls unconscious instantly and dies in a matter of seconds.

It may sound a little gross, but it's a heck of a lot faster than I've seen some people go. Anyway, this guy's hair was all messed up; he had been pulling on it with his hands. But now, he seemed to be a little more at peace since the medication was taking effect. He looked to be about 40 or

42, sandy blond hair, trim build, and a red face on which, every once in a while, a tear would run down. He really didn't want to die, but the medication was kind of screwing him up now and keeping him from thinking about that. He looked around; he looked at me several times. They always look at you when you're in uniform; in a situation like this, they always look at you with those searching, peering, prying eyes, trying to find out if there is something you can do. I was a lot younger than anyone there. Heck, I was the youngest guy there. In fact, I think the next youngest to me was maybe ten years older than I was. Yet it was just given and understood that I was running the show, to some extent—that is, after the doctor and now the ambulance drivers, who were walking up and did all they could do. We just stood back and waited for the remains.

I could hear a group of people walking from a distance, getting closer to us. I could hear the stones shuffling under their feet as they were coming down the stony path. Every once in a while, I could hear a whimper coming from the direction of the people who were approaching. I could hear a woman crying, I could hear a little child crying. It's his family. His family is here now. Everyone standing around, myself included, tried not to let our eyes meet the wife's, the guy who was dying, or especially the little kid's eyes. We sure as heck didn't want them to see us and maybe ask us for help. What were we going to do? We were about as helpless as someone falling off a building. We were falling, and falling; there's not a darn thing we could do about that, and neither was there anything we could do about this. Not a thing!

His wife came up and hugged him. She walked up to him, put her arms around him, and hugged him. She was crying. Her blouse was full of blood now from his shirt and a sheet covered with blood. Someone had wrapped a sheet around his torso, trying to keep the blood in, but it was oozing out. It was a nice hot night, and blood seemed to want to flow more on those hot nights. The colder it is, the less blood you have coming out of a wound. He was talking a little slurred; I think that was more from the medication than his injuries. He didn't complain of pain now. His wife and kids were crying. There was another guy with them; I don't know who he was, but obviously, he was a friend of the family, or maybe a brother of hers or something like that. The kids called "daddy" several times, but the woman wouldn't let them go up and see this guy in the coupled cars. He asked to see them, and this friend of the family, who was a big man himself with tears in his eyes, carried the kids up to see their daddy one last time.

A cute little boy and girl, if I had to guess, I would say they were about 6 or 7 years old, maybe even a little younger. They seemed so helpless now; they couldn't believe what was going on. Hell, I don't blame them; I couldn't believe it either. What kind of business would you have where you just accept the fact that one of your employees could be killed between two cars and you set something up to get his family out there so they can say goodbye to him? Everybody accepted it, why can't I? Why can't I accept it?

Each of these little kids kissed their dad on his cheek, began crying, and then this friend of the family carried them away. The three of them, the two kids and the friend, all crying as he set the kids down by the wife. They held onto her skirt, legs, and waist as they cried out of control. She put one hand on each of their heads and cried herself, telling them not to cry. The guy who had just carried the children must have been more than a friend; he must have been some relation himself because he walked back up to the dying man and told him, as he knelt by his dying friend, that he would take care of his wife and kids. He said, "Don't worry about Janie and the children, I'll take care of them." "Thank you," in a weak voice, the dying man softly said. This friend or relative, whoever he was, leaned over and kissed his friend on the cheek. Now, if you saw a guy kiss another guy on the street, you would think there was something wrong with him, but under these circumstances, it was a very emotional thing, a tearing situation; everyone had tears in their eyes.

The doctor started to listen to his heart again and asked him how he felt. He didn't answer him. His arms weren't moving much now. I guess the medication was getting to him, or he was that low on blood, or maybe a combination of both. That's probably it! He was leaning over to his left, kind of slouching down on the coupling itself, half on that coupling that was squeezing the life out of him. His knees were bent and twisted to the side, where now a lot of blood began to run down, dripping to the ground. There was a puddle down there. You could see a pool of his blood on the rocks, stones, and on one of the railroad ties. He wanted another cigarette and asked us to please make his wife and kids leave. She ran over and gave him a kiss, and he told her to go. She shook her head no and kept backing up away from him. She turned, ran back to her friend, and started crying as they took the children back down the tracks. I never saw them again, and I'm glad of that. I didn't want to see the pain on her face again. I didn't even know this guy, and I was feeling pain in my heart, that aching feeling, the same feeling I get every time I feel helpless.

"Well, Bill, it's time now. Do you want to wait a little bit longer?" "No," he mumbled. Obviously, this was a close friend of his. He took the cigarette from his friend's mouth and threw it to the ground. Bill said, "I'm ready." About three people asked, "Are you sure you're not hurting anywhere, Bill?" "I'm not feeling anything. All I feel is good and dizzy. You guys make sure Jane's okay and the kids," he asked.

I didn't hear any reply at first. As I looked around, I could see heads shaking "yes," and someone forced out a "yes." He looked up, wide-eyed. He knew that they all would, and he also knew that they couldn't talk. He knew it hurt them too much, and they didn't want to start crying. He smiled and said, "Let's get this shit over with."

The engine was running some distance down the tracks; the ground rumbled from its power. One guy held onto the coupling bar, or decoupling bar, whichever it was going to be. This guy was going to pull it and unlock the coupler. Another guy talking into a radio told the engineer to start easing forward. You could hear clicking down the line of the couplings on the other cars, coming together and taking up the slack. It sounded like giant dominos falling, "bang! bang! bang!" This sound started out way in the distance and was getting closer and closer, louder and louder.

I don't know how in the heck this guy knew when to pull that bar; the tears were coming down his face so fast, but he did. It seemed like a second before that banging reached the car which brutally held the body of his friend, he pulled the bar. The combination of him pulling it and releasing the coupling and the train moving forward about 7 or 8 feet caused this guy to fall lifelessly to the ground. The doctor and another guy ran over to the horizontal victim and turned him over; as they did, there was no sign of life, his body moved like a ragdoll.

The doctor, with his stethoscope in hand, listened to Bill's heart, or where it should have been beating. He just kept shaking his head "no," as if he was giving us a blow-by-blow description of what was happening. We knew he was dead. It would have been a heck of a surprise to me if he wasn't. I didn't see as many of these as the other guys did, and I knew he was dead. He just laid there for a little bit. The paramedic walked by and asked me if it was alright to remove the body. I told him to talk to the doctor first.

I asked if anyone had actually seen the accident happen. No one said they did. I asked who was running the train. "That guy down there crying," someone told me and pointed in the direction of a man sitting on the ground with his head in his hands. I'm not going to talk to him now.

"Can anybody tell me how they knew this guy was trapped between these cars?" "Well, officer," one of the guys replied, "they were switching, and they lost communication with him, so they stopped the train. They thought maybe he wasn't feeling good and started walking back down the line. Another switchman on one side and the engineer on the other, as they walked back, they were calling to him. One of them heard him moaning in between the cars. As he looked in between them, he didn't realize he was coupled between the cars; he thought maybe he was just leaning against the coupling. It was so dark you couldn't see." Whoever it was that first found him yelled to the other one to go get a flashlight. After he brought the lantern back, he saw the horrible sight of him hanging there. As he hung, it appeared that he was holding his breath; he could take little gasps of air, gasping slowly, letting it in, and hardly letting it out.

I found out later that the guy who died may have come to work with too much to drink. He had a bit of a drinking problem and always drank a little on the job. He made a mistake and had the train back up, and at the last minute, he saw that the other coupling wasn't right. He didn't think it would couple correctly, so he was trying to grab it and push it over. Those train cars, in the dark, rolling so slowly, make no noise at all. They're like a cat walking in the dark; the only difference is they're deadly. Deadly and they have no mercy, no feelings whatsoever.

After they removed the body from between the tracks, I got all of my information from a couple of guys who had their faculties about them. I walked back to the squad car thinking about my family and what it would be like if I got shot, was dying, and we had a policy where they would call my family to the scene.

Would I want them to be there?

Would I want them to see me that way?

What could I say?

Could I say the same things that this guy said?

He told her something about wanting the kids to finish school. What would your last words be? What's important enough to talk about before you die? What are things that aren't important enough?

I don't know. I'm not afraid of dying; I'm afraid of suffering. I don't know what I would say to my loved ones. I don't know what I would say to my friend. You'd have to weigh your words.

"A dying request is taken by some people to be solid and firm, something that they have to live by. Is that fair to them? Is it fair to tie them down with something?"

"And you sure as heck don't want to be a martyr. 'Forget me, remarry' - if you tell them that, then what are you, a martyr?"

I think it's better not to have anyone around. I think it would be better to die alone. Have your loved ones remember you the way you are living now? But then again, it was his choice. For those hours, he was all that mattered to anyone who was there. The trains didn't move at all that night, as I recall; it was a kind of silent vigil that they kept in memory of him. The next day, however, it was "business as usual." The same trains crept down the tracks, steel against steel, so precisely made that the wheels and the tracks met each other and made that little rumble as they went by, but nothing to announce their approach.

"Maybe if there had been something like that, he wouldn't have gotten between the couplings. Or maybe if he hadn't been drinking, he wouldn't have stepped between the couplings, or maybe if they devised a new way of switching cars, he wouldn't have had to be between the cars at all."

But a week later, it was total "business as usual," except for some haunting memories. No one mentioned anything about it, especially the company; they were probably just concerned about being sued by the family. No one wanted to talk about it. No one there that night, no one around it - heck, people just want to forget these things. I don't blame them, and neither do I. I suppress my feelings on a daily basis doing this job. What a memory it must have left for those kids, to see their dad like that.

I don't care what anyone says; I don't think it's right. Now I have to go back to work, trying to clean the mud off my shoes and pants so I can take some calls that may seem to be a little worthless. However, to those who call, the problems are serious. You try to act as if you were just waiting for them to call and do the best you can to help them. Maybe that will help me remember that just because I couldn't do anything to help the last guy, helping someone now can make me feel worth a little more.

Chapter 4
The Hidden Hydrant

It's the midnight shift, and I'm so tired my eyes are burning.

The car is feeling its way down the road, and I'm hoping I don't drift off to sleep and end up in the ditch, like Johnson did last week, a few blocks from where I am now.

I have the radio turned up, and the window open, and I'm singing, trying to stay awake.

Just as I think I'm going to fall asleep, a guy appears in the road in front of my car. He's waving his arms as if there's an emergency. As I slow down, I tell my partner to be careful since I don't know why this guy is flagging us down.

"What does he want?" Bill asked. "Officer, the house over there is on fire!" he yelled, pointing to a newer home with smoke seeping out from the roof.

We called it in and asked for the fire department to be sent as we got out of the car and ran to the front door. Pounding on the door and then opening it, I saw smoke rushing out at me. I went in and yelled for anyone who might still be inside the home.

There was no answer. The entire first floor was covered with a cloud of heavy black smoke. My first breath brought with it intense burning to my nose and a stabbing pain in my head, as if it were going to explode. It felt as though someone had packed red-hot cotton into my throat. My throat instantly became dry, swollen, and painful, making it hard to swallow. My eyes fought me as I tried to open them and expose them to the irritating air. As I opened them, I could see my partner, all 230 pounds of him, on his hands and knees, crawling in slow motion and holding the stair rail as he ascended the steps. He was choking so badly I thought he was either crying or dying; I couldn't tell which. I was sure I was close to death myself as I ran out the door, gasping for clean air. My partner came out after me, like a "zombie," and fell to his knees in the front yard.

I asked if he saw anyone in the house, and he said he didn't, but he couldn't get upstairs to check the bedrooms. As we left the home, we closed the front door, thinking it would be better than giving the building more air for combustion.

Another guy approached and said, "I'm a fireman from North Town. Is everyone out of the home?" I told him we didn't know since we couldn't get in due to the heavy smoke. He said, "I'm getting my gear to go in and check to see if anyone is inside, if that's okay with you." I agreed, and as I called to check on the fire units and get an ETA, the North Town fireman returned with his gear. He had a face mask and a small tank on his back as he went inside with our blessing. He came back out very quickly and reported to us, as if we had sent him on a mission and he was now briefing us.

"Three bedrooms, I checked them all. No one was under or in the beds. No one in the closets," he reported. He might have said some other things, but I wasn't paying much attention after he indicated that the house was empty. I was too preoccupied with my own problems.

It felt like I had hornets stinging my throat and nose, and I thought I was dying. The city fire truck arrived and prepared to fight this burning "smokehouse". The North Town fireman told our city firemen the same thing he told us.

The Captain and some other firemen looked at him first, as if they didn't know what the heck he was talking about. Later, it seemed as if he had infringed upon their private war and was no longer welcome in their presence. They exchanged several words, and the North Town guy left in a rage, yelling back some parting obscenities.

The front door of the home, the one my partner, the North Town fireman, and I had opened to enter the home, was closed after the North Town fireman came back out.

Without turning the doorknob, a husky city fireman, dressed in a red helmet, and a black raincoat, and brandishing a very large and lethal-looking ax, began to hit the front door with the ax as if he were trying to knock the door down and through the house with one swing. As splinters flew from the door, and after this guy stopped losing his footing and almost falling, he finally succeeded in leveling one of the double, unlocked doors. Upon completing his task, he looked back at his comrades as if to solicit approval or maybe an ovation.

He smiled as two other firemen, dressed in heavy coats and face masks, made their way into the home. A second fire truck arrived, which was another pumper. A pumper is a truck that carries its own supply of water and can also use hose hook-ups to fire hydrants. They began to work on the rear roof, which now had small flames licking from the lowest point. The other truck dropped lines and hooked up to a hydrant about a block away.

As they watered down the home, the flames seemed to increase. The second truck, after using its supply of water, was as useless as an empty glass. Its firefighters, looking lost and frustrated, noticed a garden hose lying on the east side of the home. I noticed it almost the same moment as the first two firemen did. As one pointed to it and talked to yet another fireman, I couldn't believe what was about to happen. Yes, they did, they turned that hose on and, as if watering some flowers, began to squirt the flames that had matured to a very large and threatening size. I couldn't help it; I laughed.

Just the sight of these guys dressed in those heavy and official-looking coats, caps, and boots, holding the skinny garden hose, was too much. One of the area chiefs walked by, and I asked why they were using that hose. Indignantly, he replied, "They're out of water in the truck they came in, and the other truck is using the only close hydrant." After hearing this, my partner asked, as he pointed to our right, "Why can't they use this one?" He was pointing to a hydrant that was only a few feet from where we were standing. This house was now totally engulfed in flames, and the roof was "falling in" in a steady progression. The noise of the falling roof sounded somewhere between that of a tree falling or a car crash. Even so, its sound was unique to itself. This fire chief said, "Oh crap! Don't show that to anyone, darn!" He muttered as he walked away, got into his car, and drove off, as if to say "out of sight, out of mind" or maybe out of trouble. Some civil defense units were on the scene directing traffic.

Since there was no need for us to stay, the radio sent us on a call where someone was breaking into a home, but that's another story.

Chapter 5
Cold Facts

It's so cold; I'm freezing in this car. The heater is on as high as it can go, and still, it's too cold. I felt like a popsicle when I left for work this morning. Well, they're sending me to check on some guy who is trying to break into a home. Five in the morning and it's so cold that my breath is freezing on my mustache, and someone is breaking into a house? No way!

Another car and I from the South beat area are going to check it out, though. As we do, more calls come in about a fight in the street and someone yelling for help. This sounds more like a 5 p.m. call in this kind of weather, I thought.

As I pull onto the street, everything is quiet and peaceful. The snow-covered road makes the car seem to float down the road. The only sound, soft and low, is that of my tires crushing the snow beneath them. I turn off my headlights and creep slowly into the approximate area of the last call for this disturbance. The road is bordered by mounds of white, fluffy snow which releases some of its powdery substance into the air as a breeze blows over them.

Except for the blowing snow, nothing moves on this picturesque street. In the distance, I see someone running as if being chased. He crawls over piles of snow, stands up, only to fall again, and acts as though he's going crazy. He's about 18 years old, medium build, with brown hair. His entire body, exposed to the cold air, is very red, as if burned. He's wearing only a T-shirt and pants. That's right, no shoes, socks, coat, or hat. He's dying from the cold. I stop the car, and he "charges" at me, screaming, "Help me!" as he begs me to let him into my car. I let him in the front seat and turn the heat up on bi-level so that it hits him chest-high as it blows out of the dash vents.

He tells me that he was drinking the night before and fell asleep in the backseat of his friend's car. He woke up freezing and got out to go into his friend's house, but he couldn't find it. He was lost and tried to get someone to let him in so he could warm up. Every door he pounded on either didn't answer his pleas for help or refused to let him in.

He's crying now, saying he can't feel anything in his feet or hands. I call for an ambulance, but he refuses to go with them. I take him to his house, where his parents let us in and can't believe what has happened.

He's drunk, scared, and freezing. I tell his parents to put him in a warm tub of water, which they do. His parents are the typical "MOM and DAD" type. I talk him into going to the hospital, where they have to warm him up from the inside out. That's something to see. They insert a tube into his stomach, fill it with warm liquids, and then remove the liquid. They keep doing this until his body temperature returns to normal. Just the sight of people lying with tubes in their noses was too much for me, so I left and tried to find somewhere warm.

Cars, radios, nothing wants to work; everything is breaking down from the cold. I don't want to do much more; it's too cold for me, so I go into the station and type some reports that I had been putting off for just such an occasion.

That doesn't last long, as there's a car accident with possible injuries that they want me to check on. Off into the cold again...

Chapter 6
16 Cars

"Car 40, we're getting numerous calls about a bad accident on Holiday Avenue by Johnson Park," the radio called out. I acknowledged and started for the location. It was a hot and humid night. The air felt thick and stagnant. As I drove to the scene, I thought to myself, "The roads are dry, and traction is good; there's no traffic light there." It was unusual to have any accident in that area, let alone a serious one. Other cars arrived on the scene and called the radio to advise them that there were about 16 cars involved in this accident.

Now, without ice, snow, or even water on the road, this didn't seem possible. When I pulled up, I could see cars parked along the east curb of Holiday Avenue by Johnson Park. They looked like they had all been pulled, twisted, and smashed into. They all had various types of damage ranging from minor scrapes to missing bumpers. A quick glance revealed a wide range of makes, models, and years of cars sitting at the curb damaged.

Some of them were out in the street more than others and most with pieces missing. "Hey, buddy," one officer said to me, smiling. "You're going to love this one! The driver is over there around the corner with Davis." "He's drunk out of his mind too," he finished as he walked away laughing.

I drove past this display of violated transports in a slow, unbelieving manner, as if I was inspecting some display arranged just for me. It was, I guess. I turned the corner to find a newer Chevy Caprice, a two-door station wagon stopped in front of two marked police cars with their red lights flashing. As I got out of the car, two officers were laughing because they knew this investigation was going to take several hours to complete. They were just giving me the business.

I walked by these "city comedians" and up to the driver of the car. He was sitting behind the wheel, staring out through the windshield, mesmerized. I opened the door of his car and asked him to step out. As he got out, I came face-to-face with this guy for the first time. He stood about 5' 10", was around 50 years old, kind of heavy-set, with his white dress shirt hanging half out of his black dress pants. His face was round and chunky, he was clean-shaven, and his face was very red and flushed-looking. As he stood out of the car, leaning against the side of it for support, he began to gasp for air at irregular intervals. From the street side, his car didn't look like it had any damage. When I walked to the right, curb-side, however, it looked like it had been dragged on its side down the road. I was angry because of all the damage this guy caused, but after talking to him, I felt a little sorry for him.

He told me that he was single and not much of a "ladies' man." However, he met a lady this evening, had dinner with her, and had a few too many drinks. Since they met at a restaurant and both had their own cars, he was on his way to her home when he misjudged and hit the cars. He was unable to stand without help, and he could not perform any of the field sobriety tests. He was taken to the station by one of the beat cars. I finished recording the information about the cars involved in the accident and went into the station to talk to the driver further. He agreed to take a chemical test, a breathalyzer, to determine if he was impaired. The results indicated that he had enough "blood alcohol" in his system to make four men or women impaired. I charged him with operating a vehicle while intoxicated.

During our conversation, I asked him if he had a drinking problem. My experience tells me that had he not been a "seasoned drinker," he would have been very sick. It was obvious to me that he had been drinking heavily for many years. He admitted that he had a problem and began to cry out of frustration and fear about the consequences of this accident. He worried about losing his job, being embarrassed when people he knew found out, and the possibility of losing his license or going to jail.

I talked to him for a while and explained that he would be out of jail in time for work on Monday. Regarding his embarrassment about the incident, I told him that he should not be embarrassed because alcoholism is a sickness, like diabetes, and that he needed to make a commitment to himself to stop drinking. I advised him to hire an attorney and attend an Alcoholics Anonymous meeting that was coming up the next week. He took my advice, as his lawyer called me to say that they both went to the AA meeting and that his client couldn't understand why I cared enough to try and help him. The charge of OWI was never contested. He pleaded guilty, and as was customary for first offenses where the arrested is getting treatment, he was placed on probation.

I haven't seen him since the arrest, and I always wonder if I made a difference in his life, or, should I say, if the way I treated him made a difference. I thought about going into the store where he works to say hi, but I wouldn't want him to think that I was checking up on him because I didn't trust him. I am just interested and concerned.

You see, if no one tries to help someone in this position, it could turn into a more serious situation later. Ten minutes later, the same street would have been filled with people going to those cars and standing next to them. Sideswiping 15 cars could have been much worse. There could have easily been multiple fatalities along with the damaged cars. I had a guy involved in an accident where a little girl was killed, and he had prior arrests and stops by policemen while he was drunk. He was either let go, taken home, or charges dropped by fancy legal maneuvering a total of 17 times. After this fatal accident, his lawyer refused to represent him. He is currently serving 20 years for reckless homicide and causing death while intoxicated. Everyone was lost in that situation—the parents, the child, and the drunk driver.

That driver was trained by the system, his friends, and his lawyer on how to beat that system and get away with driving drunk. Society, by having to care for, feed, and house this drunken driver, lost too. No one won! I did not want this guy to wind up the same way.

Chapter 7: Scared! Why?

Working patrol, I was sent to a basement apartment of a house regarding a family fight where the male involved had a gun and was threatening to kill his wife. When I arrived, two other officers were on the scene, waiting for me. We were let in by the family upstairs, who warned me to be careful because the "guy is crazy" and has a gun. While walking down this narrow, dark stairway, I called ahead, "Joe, this is Corporal Thomas of the Police Department. I want to talk to you." "I don't want to talk to you, man. It's none of your business." "I agree," I said, "just let us see your wife, find out you guys don't need us, and we'll get out of here, okay?"

As I walked into the small, cramped room, I asked Joe if he had a gun and began patting him down with my left hand as he stood in the center of the room. My other hand was on my gun. This room was so small that the other two officers had to stand on the steps because there was not enough room for them in the room where we were standing. As I talked to Joe and patted him down, I heard a loud bang. A firecracker, I thought? "This makes me crazy," went through my mind as my ears hurt and began ringing.

As I turned to look behind me, I saw a woman with a gun pointed right at my stomach. My eyes fixed on this gun as it fired a second time. I was so sure that I was shot I looked down to see where I was hit. I felt no pain, but I also knew that when your adrenaline is pumping so high and fast, a lot of times you don't always feel pain right away. My eyes no sooner saw my stomach when my mind screamed, "NO! SHOOT BACK!"

Automatically, I pulled my gun and began to fire back. As I did, she fired a third time and disappeared into a small room from where she had appeared from. I had fired three times at her, during which time her husband hit the ground to avoid being shot. I yelled into the room, "Come out with your hands up." "I can't, I'm shot," a voice moaned from the room. I went into the room and found out that she was, in fact, hit twice: once in the arm and once in her leg. I took the gun and called for an ambulance.

While waiting for the ambulance, I checked the shirt I was wearing for holes or wet spots but couldn't find any. I pushed on my stomach and chest but could find no sore spots where I may have been shot. After leaving the scene, I went into the station, stood in front of a mirror, and took off my shirt. This way, I thought, I could see any red blood spots on my white T-shirt easier. I was so sure that I had been hit at least once, but I wasn't.

The other two officers asked how I kept so calm. All I could tell them was that I didn't have time to be scared. I did get nervous later, however, but not about the woman who was shooting at me. No, it was from listening to one of the officers who was behind me at the time. He said he almost got a shot off at her with his sawed-off shotgun but didn't because my head kept getting in the way. That statement made me more nervous than the shots fired by the lady.

I always ask God to protect me in such matters, and He always did and still does! Isaiah 54:17 says, "No weapon formed against you shall prosper." I have prayed this verse many times in times of danger.

Chapter 8
The Curve

I'm driving down this lonely road, heading westbound. It's the middle of the night, I'm tired, and I'm driving so I won't fall asleep. There is a guy riding with me, a friend, and someone I have known for most of my life. In fact, we grew up together in a small town just south of where I'm now working. I have been in the Police Department for several years, and this friend of mine, Bob, was on the County Police. He had only been in the County for about six months. We were talking about the usual things, telling each other stories about good arrests we made, each bragging about our own department. "I just quit smoking last week," he told me. He knew I would like to hear that, as I don't smoke and never could stand it.

We were going westbound and approaching a sharp curve in the road. The curve wasn't hard to make, but if ever I saw a curve that could have been named after that one they sing about in the song "Dead Man's Curve," well, this was it. We had a lot of people killed there, or should I say coming up to it, at it, or going away from it. Most of them just forgot to slow down or turned too late when they came up to it. Some had too much to drink or maybe fell asleep. The results were the same; they either hit someone else or they hit that darn building that someone decided to stick there for the electrical transformers.

As we approached it, I thought about how much we were at the mercy of the oncoming traffic. If they go left of center and we're right in the middle of the turn, there is a guardrail that keeps you from going off the road to avoid a crash. Big problem, or maybe the end of all of our problems. Anyhow, I was into the turn when I saw a car coming the other way. This car was flying, and I mean going like someone was chasing him. As he got close to us, he started to swerve back and forth, but not as if he was out of control, more like he was playing chicken with us.

"He is going to hit us," I said as he drove left of center and was coming right at us head-on. I pulled off the road and had the bumper of my squad up against and touching the guardrail. You know, that thing that is supposed to protect you. The same thing that now was holding the car and keeping us from getting away from this oncoming vehicle. "Oh no," Bob said as he grabbed the dash. All I could say was, "he's going to hit us." I thought to myself, is he aiming at us because we're in a police car? Maybe he'll pull it off because of that fact. I just sat there waiting for that racing blur of steel to hit and kill us. Maybe that car or steel was "hexed" with a curse and must kill police officers in uniform, and it was about to fulfill its mission. Funny how crazy thoughts run through your mind at a time like that.

For some reason, I thought that if I turned on our red lights, they might see us and get back on their side of the road. You know, you can really think up some crap when you're scared. I did turn on the red lights and just before this modern-day "kamikaze" hit us, he pulled back onto the road from where he came and over to his side, still going fast enough to qualify for the Indianapolis 500 race.

In a heartbeat, our fear of death passed, and in its place came anger. We made a U-turn and chased that car like nothing else mattered; at that point, it didn't. When we stopped him, he was crying and drunk. He had a young child in the car with him, and he told us that he was going to kill himself and the lad but didn't want to hurt a policeman. Thank the Lord for that! If we would have been in our own cars, we would have been all over the road now. We sent this guy to the mental health department of the local hospital for an evaluation.

After doing all of the reports, I noticed that Bob was smoking a cigarette. He said that this was just the "encouragement" he needed to get back in the swing of things. Smoking, that was. He smoked for some years after that, but I'd say, in the last five years or so, he has quit again. I think he won't start up again; you see, he married a young lady that does not like smoking either. Then again, it's easy for him now because he never travels down the road that goes around "the curve."

Chapter 9: I Couldn't Stop Crying

While working accident investigation one day, I saw the saddest situation of my life. Being sent to an accident with injuries, I called ahead on the radio directing other officers who were on scene to do certain things and secure the crash site. Upon arriving, I saw seven police officers walking around; some were helping ambulance personnel remove the injured people from a car, while others rushed up to me as if to relieve themselves of the information they had collected. Most of all, they wanted to be "released" from the call so they could leave and go anywhere else. You see, there was a six-year-old child killed in this accident. Other traffic officers arrived, and I assigned them to various tasks such as taking pictures, taking measurements, and talking to the witnesses.

I looked on as this little girl was taken from the car. "So pretty and peaceful," I thought as I saw her right profile. As her face came fully round and exposed to my view, I could see that the left side was gone, removed by the impact of the truck. I have investigated hundreds of accidents, and the damage I saw to this car was minor. By no means did it seem right, I thought, as I walked up closer to the child. My mind raced faster and faster. "This can't be right; it's a mistake. Somehow or someway I should be able to change this. She can't be dead. It's not right! It's just not right!"

"Oh, my baby," a cry rang out. The mother fell and hit the ground with her hands. Yes, she had just seen that which I will never forget. "I'll kill that son-of-a-bitch," a voice yelled out from a passing man running across the lanes of traffic, making his way for the driver of the pickup truck. "Stop him," I yelled to some officers. As they grabbed him, he began to cry and fell to the ground, unable to stand. Looking back at the child, a paramedic looked at me and gave "that sign," a head shake no, which I had seen many times on other calls. It meant no signs of life at all and no practical way to revive them. D.O.A., I still did not believe what I was seeing. The child on the ground looked just like my daughter: same size, same color of hair, and same little hands with fingernail polish on her fingernails.

"Corporal Thomas," a cry went out in a voice that startled me. It was the mother yelling to me, asking me to please come over to her. I later found out one of the other officers told her I was in charge. I went up to her, and she asked me please not to let the man who killed her baby go. "I won't, ma'am," I replied. An officer ran up to me, pulled on my arm with unreal strength, and said, "She's dead; she was dead when we took her out. I'm telling you she's dead." "Just relax," I said, "go over with Johnson, and help him direct traffic on the north end." He ran to that location. I could not feel my feet as I walked. The sweat was running off my face so fast it seemed like rain. I felt like I was going to explode. I was in control; even though I had these thoughts, I was still functioning and not crying. I had been on the scene for under two minutes; it seemed like years of hard labor.

I walked up to the driver of the truck, who was still sitting in the driver’s seat. As I approached him, he looked at me and asked, "Do you want me out?" "Yes, would you stand over here and give me your driver's license?" I replied. He got out of the truck and fell to the ground. As I helped him back up, I could smell beer on his breath. Yes, he was loaded. Knowing my obligations well in these situations, I informed him of his rights. The crowd that had gathered was becoming loud and angry as cries directed at this man were being yelled. "I need a two-man unit to take an arrested subjwect to the station," I called.

Two officers came up just as the child's father came up crying out, "Hey man, look what you've done to my kid." I grabbed the father and returned him to the ambulance, as the drunken driver was taken into the station. "The pictures are done; here's the film," one officer said as he walked up to me. "Measurements are done," another said. "Do you want the witnesses in the station now?" "No, they can go; they already said they will come in tomorrow for written statements. I already have their verbal ones," I answered.

I was finished at the scene, and now it was time to go to the hospital, get the names and ages, and find out the type of injuries the people had that were taken there from the accident. For the first time in over 13 years, I just could not do it. I knew I had to get somewhere, anywhere, alone because I was ready to break. The traffic lieutenant was on the scene, and I asked him to go to the hospital and get the necessary information. He agreed immediately, as he knew I had a good reason for asking him to do it. I went right into the station, past about 20 people, officers, and civilians who were asking what happened. I went into the traffic bureau without talking to any of them. Never before in my life had I been so driven to find a place to go and cry.

It must have shown; as I walked past the captain, into his office, and straight ahead into his private restroom, which usually is reserved for supervisors only, everyone gave me a "wide berth." Once inside, the tears came out fast and steady. I cried so hard my eyes hurt from squinting. I exhaled so long that I had to gulp for air, and then it was only a second or two before another cry began. The thing that hurt me most was thinking this little girl riding in her daddy's car must have thought, "I'm with mommy and daddy, and nothing can hurt me; they won't let it." I stayed in that room for a long time. It didn't seem long to me. When I did come out, everyone was extra nice to me. I guess they knew the hurt I felt. I don't think about it too often anymore, but when I do, I still have tears come to my eyes and pain in my heart. It wasn't long before I left the traffic division and went into criminal investigation.

Chapter 10: Her Sadness Was Too Much

"Patrol car 4," the radio operator called in an overly solemn tone. "4 clear," I answered quickly and in an equally serious manner; I could sense something serious in the radio operator's voice. "Johnson and the expressway, we've got numerous calls about a woman who just jumped onto the expressway." "Ten-four," I responded as I turned on the red lights and siren. "We've got an ambulance en route also, car 4." "Ten-four," I answered back.

When I arrived, nothing was moving eastbound on the expressway, and hundreds of people were out of their cars, standing in the once-heavily-traveled lanes of this expressway. As I pulled up within five hundred feet of the largest group, some people were waving at me to stop fast. I braked, and the car slid on the pavement. I thought, at first, the road was wet with oil or water, maybe. I found out as I got out of the car that I was slipping and almost falling as I tried to stand on something red and very slippery. The covering had a color somewhere between clear and red. I found out later it was the remains of that woman who jumped and was hit by a truck.

Her body was dragged against the asphalt and became a twisted mess of flesh and clothing, one hardly distinguishable from the other. No matter their ages, people at the scene of something like this always look at you as if you have all the answers. I don't mind that most of the time, but when I feel this helpless myself, I hate it. You have to function, or mechanically do the things you must, and bring an end to the disorder. You do the tasks that bring back order.

This scene was really bad, people crying, cops turning from the sight in shock, and most looking at you as if you arrived with a "bag of answers." From the start, you learn that your feelings, or more so emotions, are not to be shown. They must be pushed back, kicked aside, or somehow shipped home until you get there later to experience them. As this crumpled mass of once-human remains lay on the street, someone walks up with a blanket and covers it in a gentle and ritualistic manner.

One of the officers starts to direct a lane of traffic, and as the cars move by, the occupants look over at you first as if they're angry about the delay. Then, when their eyes grasp the blanket laid reverently on that mound, they instinctively know what it conceals, and their look changes to one of concern and sorrow. They ask themselves if it's someone they know, someone they're related to, or someone they've ever seen. They send all the looks in rapid glances. Back to the business at hand, find the witnesses, get their names, and get a statement as to the exact sequence of events.

"Tom, is this yours?" an officer asks as I walk by. "I don't think so," I reply, my eyes fixed on a problem that has, up to this point, been overlooked by everyone at the scene. This problem was a man who was sitting in the first police car crying uncontrollably. This red-faced, stout-built figure of a man who looked to be in his mid-50s was the driver of the truck that had just hit the woman. I opened the rear door of this car and asked him if he was okay.

"Is she dead? I know she has to be," he sobbed. "Come with me," I said in a sober tone. As I started to lead him from the car, an angry sergeant started half running up to me, saying, "Leave him in the car!" I kept walking and waved him closer to me and explained that I was going to put him in the furthest car from the scene. In a second, his mood changed as he patted me on the back and said he was sorry. He probably thought I was going to arrest this poor man. When we got to the last police car, I opened the door and helped him into the car. This once capable and independent man was crying or sobbing out of control. I called to the other officers at the scene and told them to send the ambulance to the car where we were at. I knew this guy was in shock and in need of help.

"Why? Why, officer? Why would she do something like that? Am I in trouble? Oh, forget that, I don't care. Just why? Why, God, why? I'm sorry, so sorry. Did you know her? Who is, was she? Please help me," he said as he fell over and lay crying on the seat.

"She looked like she was falling in slow motion. I didn't believe my eyes," he cried out. The ambulance took him to the hospital where he had a heart attack and died later that week. My job's a real slice! A young state trooper arrived and took the report as an accident. We all knew it was the wrong thing to do because it was a suicide, but that's the way things work on this job. I found out later that day that this lady had been despondent for some months after losing her son. He died in a car accident somewhere; I don't know exactly where. Her sadness was just too much for her to handle, and so she walked back and forth for hours over the bridge which covered the expressway where she, after getting enough nerve, jumped onto, and in the path of, the 18-wheeler and that poor soul driving it. We assisted the young state trooper with his report and left after the coroner removed the body to where an autopsy would take place. I went on other calls for the rest of my shift. Too many people are alone with problems, and they need help... Just sad!

Chapter 11: Dream or Not?

It begins with me in a store behind a counter and over in a secluded area. I think it's a pharmacy because the man working there is wearing a smock that looks like the ones they wear in a pharmacy. There is another employee standing by this guy, a young girl, pretty and small. Someone walks up to the counter and addresses both of them in a calm voice. “Put all the money from the register in a bag and give it to me right away.” I now realize that I am a police officer, in uniform, and this is an armed robbery in progress.

I know I can stand where I am, keep quiet, do nothing, and I will be safe and hidden until the robbery is over. If I try to stop him, he might overreact and shoot one of them. I don't know if I could live with myself. This guy starts telling the female that he is going to take her with him when he leaves. I cannot let him take her. I decided to draw my weapon, a .357 Magnum, and point it at the man with the shotgun. I know this is risky because even if I get this guy before he sees me, he may shoot and kill the girl.

I am conflicted because it just does not seem right to shoot this guy without giving him the chance to surrender. I pull the trigger, and nothing happens except the hammer hitting the frame of the gun, making a very loud noise. The man looks right at me, and now I see that there are two other guys with shotguns standing by the front door, and all of them are looking right at me. I know that I cannot survive an attack with such overwhelming firepower against me. All three have sawed-off shotguns. I'm going to have to take at least one of them out before they can react to me, or I will surely die. Now the guy I am pointing my gun at turns and points the shotgun at me.

This is one of the craziest dreams I've ever had. If I only had it one time, it would be bad; however, this dream haunts me at least once or twice a month. The incident is bad enough, but I know now that my gun is not working. So now I am just pointing a useless gun at three armed robbers. This will not end well! I wake, and as usual, feel a sense of peace. I do not know why I keep having this dream...

Chapter 12: Gang Beating Truck Driver

Only being in the department for a couple of months, I did not fully understand the relationship between the offenders, criminals, and police officers at this point. This incident offers some insight into that interaction. As we were leaving the briefing, we got a call to an intersection four blocks from the police station. The call was in regard to a gang fight in the middle of an intersection. When we arrived, there were about 15 to 20 biker gang members beating a guy who they dragged out of a pickup truck. In the cab of the truck was a woman and a child crying hysterically. The first officers who got to the group yelled for them to stop beating on this guy, but they ignored the officer and continued beating and kicking him. Additional arriving officers began to pull the gang members off of the truck driver as we tried to do when we arrived. The bikers had no reservations about hitting we officers and did so as fast as they could. About 6 others officers arrived, making a total of about 10 of us.

The fight went on for what seemed like hours when I am sure it was more like a couple of minutes. After the tide turned, the bad guys were now on the ground after getting their butts kicked by us. Being the rookie on site, I mainly was the guy that was doing the cuffing of the often motionless bad guys prostrate on the ground. This was the first time I realized that not everyone respected or feared the police. It was a matter of might being right, and the loser paid the price. It cost us also because of all the paperwork connected with these arrested guys and we took a lot of hits in the process of making the arrest.

Chapter 13: The Royal Treatment

There was a booking sergeant who was elderly, difficult, and grouchy in nature. One day while trying to book a young guy who was drunk. The guy kept grabbing at the sergeant, who was in his 60s and much smaller than the younger drunk. The sergeant just kept pushing his hands away and warning him to stop touching him. The drunk was on one side of a 4-foot counter facing the sergeant, who was on the other side of a wall. All at once, the drunk slapped the booking sergeant on the top of his head and began laughing at him. Without saying a word, the sergeant picked up the typewriter and hit the drunk in the face with it, knocking him out.

The typewriter was an old manual one made by the "Royal Manufacturing Company"; hence "the royal treatment" was adopted by the "rank and file" as a consequence of the old sergeant's anger. I had to ride in the ambulance to the ER where he was treated and released back to us. I returned this knockout victim to the booking area healed, more sober, and a little bit wiser where the booking process was completed. He was a perfect gentleman during this process. Funny how the typewriter is mightier than the sword or pen!

Chapter 14: Man Threatening Residents

While working the afternoon shift as a patrolman in Area Five, the radio received a call that there was a white male subject threatening people living in a residential area on my beat. When I arrived, I was met by several people who had called the station to report this guy. They told me that this man seemed to be either on drugs or intoxicated. They said that he had left in a green Chevy convertible. Going in the direction they said he went, I found the car abandoned in the 200 block of Oak Street. The radio received a call that a white male was trying to get into cars in the 100 block of Oak.

I found a white male lying down in the front seat of a Chevy station wagon in the 100 block of Oak Street. I opened the door and ordered him to get out of the vehicle. He got out, and I asked what he was doing. I searched him and found that he was carrying a .38 caliber revolver. I asked him if he had a permit for that weapon, and he said that he did not. I put him in handcuffs and in the back seat of my car.

I took him to the booking area where he was booked for public intoxication and carrying a pistol without a permit. After an hour and a half of doing my paperwork, I returned to continue patrolling my beat.

Chapter 15: Home Invasion or Attempted Rape

It was the midnight shift, 11 PM to 7 AM, and Bill and I were just over two hours into the shift. It was one of those hot, humid, and sticky nights where the air was so thick that it was hard to breath. Even though it was so hot and uncomfortable, we were riding with our windows down. We did this because at night it is important to hear glass breaking, someone calling out for help, or gunshots. We had the air-conditioning on as cold as it would go blowing on us to keep from overheating. The quiet night is interrupted by a siren close to where we are at this time. I call dispatch and ask if they have a report of a police chase from another city entering ours as we can hear sirens. They say no but unit four is enroute to 1142 Maple Street in regard to a rape in progress. Dispatch then calls out, "Unit five and any unit in the area of 1142 Maple we have a home invasion and rape in progress with the caller on the line at this time." "The victim got away from the rapist and is hiding in the bathroom with the door locked." We later found out that car four was dropping reports off to the dispatch/radio room when the dispatcher told them of the crime in progress. The officers left the station and were just heading to the address when we heard the sirens. When officers arrived, they determined that someone had broken into the home by the front window which was broken by this culprit. While officers arrived and began to surround the home, the husband arrived, and before anyone could stop him, he ran into the house. This guy was built like one of those guys you see on TV in the wrestling matches. He was six foot four inches tall and built like a professional weight lifter. Before officers could get into the home, there were two guys now out of an upstairs window, on the roof the one running from the other. The husband went to the upstairs bedroom where he found a male attempting to break into the adjoining bathroom to rape his wife. The homeowner chased the rapist, who ran to a window opened it, and climbed out onto the roof to get away. The husband followed onto the roof, grabbed the assailant, and literally threw him from the third-floor roof to the ground. The rapist jumped up and began to run with officers in pursuit.

This assailant was apprehended a block away without any injuries after falling three stories to the ground. All of us kept saying that if a cop fell off of that two-foot ladder, he would have died or been seriously injured. We were sent to a call about a guy looking in car windows on a residential street. We go from one adrenalin rush to another on this job.

Chapter 16: Stubborn Drunk Arrested for Public Intoxication

Dealing with drunks is one of the most frustrating jobs a police officer has to do. There was a very intoxicated person brought into the booking area, arguing with the sergeant and warden. They asked if I would help with the booking process, and I did. I kept trying to explain that he had too much to drink and we had to book him and hold him for 5 hours until he was sober. After arguing with him for at least 20 minutes, he told me that he knew we got him for something more than drinking. I finally told him that he was arrested for "attempting to assassinate the Polish ambassador to the United States." He got very serious and seemed to sober up a little. He said that he did not do it and that he was a political prisoner. He cooperated with the booking process and went to the cell without any more arguing or resistance.

The next morning, he was taken with the rest of the prisoners in the city jail before the judge for a bond hearing. The judge asked him if he knew what he was arrested for, and he said yes. He told the judge that he did not attempt to kill the Polish ambassador and he wanted a lawyer. The judge tried to tell him that he was only charged with having drank too much alcohol and was drunk. He did not believe the judge. He went on so long and argued so much that the judge sent him for a psych evaluation. He began to scream that the judge should "free his people, now!" Some of the officers laughed because they knew someone told him that he was charged with an attempt on the ambassador's life. You've got to love some of these guys both the arrested and fellow officers...

Chapter 17: Hospital's Disregard for Uninsured Person

Someone from the hospital called the radio and said that there was a trespasser in the ER that they wanted removed from their property. When I arrived, a nurse said that the administrator wanted this homeless guy arrested and removed from the property. The nurse also said that one of the doctors in the ER treated him and said he was okay. When I talked to this guy he said that he was in pain and could not walk. The hospital administrator came to the ER and told me to arrest him and get him off of the hospital property. I talked to the man, who was sitting on the floor of the outside ER doors, he said that they did not do any tests and that the doctor said that he was not going to be admitted. The guy began to cry and told me that he had no money or insurance and that is when they stopped even talking to him.

I refused to arrest the man, and the hospital big shot said he was calling the chief to get him to order me to make the arrest. I told him that was good and that while he was calling the chief, I was going to call the local news and give them the story of how you treat sick, uninsured patients. Maybe they will have a video team interview me about what you want me to do. Anyone trying to arrest a sick or injured person would not look too good on national television. After some yelling and name-calling, the hospital administrator had this man taken back inside and had another doctor examine and treat him. This big shot was angry and said that he was going to report me for not being courteous. I told him my name again and to tell the chief I said hi. His face turned bright red, and he went inside the hospital. Not often, but sometimes you can help people who would have been run over by the system. At that time we had a real no nonsense chief who never talked to me about this incident. It was good to work for someone who cared about the less fortunate people in need.

Chapter 18: Girl has Seizure and Mom Panics

A mom called us because her daughter, who was about 20 years old, broke up with her boyfriend. The guy was angry and refused to leave. We arrived, and after the mother told the boyfriend to leave in front of us, we informed him that we could now arrest him for trespassing if he did not comply. He left without incident. My partner, who was the senior officer, advised the mom and daughter to call us if he came back and not to talk to him. As my partner walked out first, the mother asked me if the guy did come back, would she have to tell him to leave again in front of us? I reassured her and her daughter not to worry, just to call us. Now that we know you do not want him here, you would not have to tell him again while we were there. We could now make the arrest based on their prior statement to us.

The daughter, who had a seizure disorder, began to shake and was sliding off the chair. As she slid off the chair, her nightgown came off, and she was completely naked on the floor. I tried to go to the door to call my partner, who was at the car by now, when the mom grabbed me, throwing me onto her naked daughter. This lady had freaky strength from fear and threw me like a ragdoll. I thought I was being set up by the two women. Mom was screaming, "Help her, help her," over and over. I said okay, but she would have to yell for my partner. I was a young officer and had never worked with this guy before. When he came back in, I was kneeling by this girl and trying to put her nightgown back on.

She finally stopped shaking and was able to get back into the chair. Later, my partner told me that when he came back in, he did not know what to think upon seeing me kneeling over this naked girl. He laughed and told me that one day I would laugh too, and that it would be a funny story to tell my grandchildren. It sure was not funny to me, at least not at that time. Ten years later, I would advise young officers to make sure to leave the call with the senior officers if they do not want to come close to having a heart attack. I get nervous and scared just remembering it, and even now as I am writing it down. Too scary for me!

Chapter 19: Woman Killed by Husband Two Times

In the detective bureau, one of the teams received a case where the husband shot his wife in the chest with a 12-gauge shotgun loaded with double-ought buckshot. She was shot at close range by her husband. The husband claimed that she was Satan because he had killed her 5 months prior, and she had come back from the dead. We thought that he was crazy. The autopsy revealed a .32 caliber bullet lodged between her skull and skin at the back of her head. When asked how he killed her before he told detectives that he had shot her in the back of the head, killing her at least 5 months before. She fell over and off the chair she was sitting in. He left and drank all night before returning home.

When he entered the home, instead of finding her on the floor, she was making breakfast for him. She complained of a very bad headache. He started shaking and thought that she was a demon coming after him. Many months later, he retrieved his shotgun and shot her in the chest with double-ought buckshot. He called the station and turned himself in because he was afraid to be home alone with her, dead or alive. Sometime the stories you hear are just too far out and hard to understand.

Chapter 20: Woman Stabbed by Husband

We were dispatched to a location where a woman was lying on the ground with a superficial knife wound. Upon our arrival, we found her on the sidewalk, crying and claiming that her husband had tried to kill her. She was awaiting an ambulance when her husband approached and inquired about her condition. Seeing him, the woman rose from the ground and grabbed him by the shirt. Weighing around 350 pounds, she forcefully slammed the man face-first into a wall. Despite his approximately 140-pound weight, he couldn't break free and began screaming for the police to intervene. We eventually convinced the woman to release him, and she sat back down on the sidewalk. When the ambulance arrived, she got up and walked to the EMTs, who placed her on a gurney and loaded her into the ambulance. After they departed, the husband got into his car and stated he was going to the hospital to check on her. We couldn't help but laugh a little. Neither one of them wanted to file charges against the other, so we finished our paperwork and left the scene and waited for a fight call to come from the hospital ER. For some reason that call did not come.

Chapter 21: Being a Young Police Officer

For many years, from my youth through my time in the army, I always wanted to be a police officer. As a young child, there was a loud noise in our basement. My father, a very fit and capable man, called the police, thinking someone had broken into the basement. There were eleven children whom my dad kept together in one room while he guarded the basement door until the police arrived. The first officer arrived and, upon hearing that someone may be in the basement, removed the chain from the door and asked my dad to inform the other officer, who was on the way, that he was downstairs. The other officer arrived, and like the first officer, immediately went down to join his partner. It was at that moment I knew I wanted to be the one who "went into the basement" to protect others.

Working various jobs as a young man and then serving in the army, I never found the satisfaction I knew I would find by "running toward the danger." Upon leaving the service, I applied to police departments and worked security jobs while waiting to be called by one of the departments I applied for. I married and had a child, and when the baby fell and injured himself, I rushed my wife holding the child in my car to a clinic that was closing for the night. A nurse leaving the clinic told us we needed to take our son to the hospital ER for treatment. Even though the baby was not in distress, I was driving as fast as I could when a police officer stopped me for speeding. He asked why I was driving so fast, and I told him what had happened. This officer said the phrase that I lived by for my twenty years as a police officer.

"I don't know if you are telling me the truth or not, but I am going to let you go. Just slow down and be careful, as you do not need to get into a car accident on your way to get help." He put the safety of my son before anything else. I was impressed.

As a young officer, I wanted to rush to danger, stop rapists, armed robbers, and so on. Being sent to check for injuries at a car accident scene, helping people who were broken down, and going to assist at homes where someone had died and needed help were distractions and not what I wanted to do—or at least, I thought!

After being on the force for several years, the light in my mind turned on, and I realized how important those distractions were. I realized that while stopping crime was important, so was helping people at their lowest and most vulnerable points.

Helping injured accident victims and ensuring the ambulance was en route was important. Helping the family whose baby died while in bed was important too. Helping the family whose loved one died in a fall was equally important. Assisting the elderly husband whose wife died in her sleep was important. Being at the home, ensuring the safety of the home and the man as they tried to move forward in this time of need, became monumentally important. On one of these calls, I asked the man, who had just lost his wife, if he would like me to call a funeral home for him. He responded by placing his hand on mine and, with his other hand, giving me a paper with the name and number of the funeral home they used. For hours, he held onto that note while the coroner checked the body and spoke to the deceased's doctor, ultimately releasing the body. He knew the love of his life was gone, but he just could not make the call, as that would be confirmation of this unthinkable nightmare.

I also called his children, giving them the news and telling them that I would stay until they arrived. I cannot describe the depth of sorrow in his eyes and how it turned to gratitude as we waited for the funeral home workers and his son to arrive.

Later, as a police officer, I mentored many officers, teaching them the importance of what I once felt was a distraction. It was not that stopping crime was not still a goal, but helping those who were down and out was just as important and occurred more often, for which I was happy to do!

Chapter 22: Working in Law Office for Many Years After Retirement

When I retired from the police department, I took a job as an investigator with a local law firm that handled personal injury cases. As an investigator, I handled all the work on cases that I could legally do without being an attorney. I was one of five full-time investigators working for the firm.

The Lord led me there for several reasons, one of which was that the senior attorney was a Jewish man who, while being a great businessman, also had a good heart. I didn't have the same training as the other investigators, but I had more experience investigating auto crashes and criminal cases, which gave me an advantage because I was good at discerning what sounded right or not. Above all, the Lord guided me while I worked on cases.

I arrived hours before everyone else and often stayed late to keep up. When I achieved great results, and the senior lawyer asked me how I did it, I told him that I prayed a lot, asking God for help. At first, he didn't know what to think, but later he told me that he knew I let God lead me and help so many people who were being treated unfairly by some insurance companies.

One time he asked me how I achieved a settlement, and I told him that I "cheated." He became very serious and asked how I did that. I explained that I asked God to put in my mind what to say and to put in the mind of the adjuster or attorney on the other side to understand and settle the case, and it worked!

One case in the office involved a truck driver who went around train gates that were down and got hit by a train. His injuries were so severe that at 45 years old, he would never be able to work again. The case was handled by the best attorney and investigator in the office. It was determined to be a case to settle for whatever we could get because it would likely be lost at trial.

The boss asked me if I would take it just to settle it for whatever I could get. Of course, I said yes, and he told me that we had the client's approval to take whatever we could get, and that I didn't have to call him. I asked the Lord for help and called the client. The client told me that if he could get a certain amount of money, he could pay off his house and live on his SSD, social security disability, with his wife.

There were three defendants against whom we had filed suit, and I was going to have to talk to all of their attorneys. I prayed hard and called all three attorneys. During a conference call with all three of them, I closed my eyes and fervently asked God to give me the words to make them want to settle the case.

I said something–I don't even remember what it was–that sounded foolish, and I thought I was ruining the case by not listening to the Lord but using my own words. There was silence for some time before I heard one attorney say, "I'll pay one-third to settle it." Immediately, another voice said, "I will pay a third," followed by a third person saying, "Well,

I am not going to be the only one to not settle." I couldn't believe what I was hearing.

They offered $150,000.00 to settle the case. I prayed and called the workers' compensation adjuster, who had a lien on the case for medical bills and other items paid, in the amount of $680,000.00. This is the amount we would have to pay back unless the adjuster for the work comp company would reduce some. I told this adjuster that we had an offer, and again, as I spoke to him, I had my eyes closed, asking the Lord to work for the good of this client and to help me get the man the money he needed.

The adjuster told me that he had informed the attorney working on the workers' comp settlement from our office that if he did not cheat him with the work comp settlement, he would be reasonable when we asked for a reduction in what we had to pay. He said that we were fair to him, and he was going to waive the entire amount. I couldn't believe what I was hearing again. I thanked the Lord for a second time.

When the boss asked me how in the world I got the settlement and the waiving of the lien, I told him that I prayed hard. He looked at me and said, "I guess prayer—no, I know prayer works because you told me so many times, and I believe you!" I never talk about all the good I did in the law office without giving credit and glory to Father God and Jesus! Without God I would not have been able to do any of the good done to help those in need....

Chapter 23: Alcohol and Society- A Policeman's View

While everyone knows something about alcohol abuse and its effects on society, no one group deals with those problems in their raw, un-subdued state more than the street police officer. These encounters range from brief confrontations to felony arrests and convictions. Even though these officers see the hazards of alcohol abuse daily, they too often fall victim to alcohol addiction themselves. It is as if society itself was the incubator of the problem and everyone in society was fair prey to its influence and domination.

Before we talk about alcohol abuse, let's answer some questions with respect to what exactly we're talking about when we use certain terms, words, and phrases. Let's start by defining what alcohol is, how it gets into the body, and how it affects the person. "Webster's New World Dictionary" describes alcohol as a "volatile, pungent, colorless liquid," which has many uses ranging from industrial to consumption. The alcohol that is used in drinks is called "ethyl alcohol." (1 Ethyl alcohol is commonly prepared for drinking by fermentation of starches, sugars, and grains. (2)

The Traffic Institute of Northwestern University's publication "Medical Effects of Alcohol" further describes ethyl alcohol as a "depressant drug" and as such, it slows mental and physical functions. (3) This classification of alcohol is also made by the "Whole College Catalog" (1976), which also describes ethyl alcohol as a drug. (4)

While there are different ways to introduce alcohol into the body, the most common is orally. Someone drinks a beer, wine, or some other form of alcoholic beverage. (1) When taken in this manner, about 20% of the alcohol enters the body from the stomach and much of the remaining 80% enters through the small intestine. (3) Other, less common, ways of introducing alcohol into the body are by taking it rectally, some type of injection, or inhaling the fumes from the alcohol. There are two effects alcohol has on the human body. One is that alcohol irritates the tissue it comes in contact with, and second, it has a sedative effect. (5) Alcohol also affects the person by relaxing their judgment and morals. (5)

As the “blood alcohol content” (BAC) increases, it affects sight, memory, reaction time, muscular coordination, and many other functions. (3) At very high BAC levels, the automatic body functions will become affected, after which death will result from respiratory paralysis. (3) The highest BAC documented was over .7%. The woman who registered at that level lived. Usually, BAC levels above .5% are serious or fatal. (3)

Our society attempts to control alcohol at every level. Alcohol control has an entire law enforcement agency to regulate and check its manufacture, sale, and use. This agency on the state level is the "State Alcoholic Beverage Commission." Federally, it is controlled by the Treasury Department, or more specifically, the "Alcohol, Tobacco, and Firearms" bureau of that department.

We, in my state, have passed laws that define "alcohol abusers" (7), "habitual substance offenders" (8), and a law that prohibits "public intoxication." (9) Lastly and most publicized are the laws that govern and control drinking and driving. In this state, it is a class "C" misdemeanor to operate a motor vehicle with ten-hundredths percent (.10%) or more by weight of alcohol in the blood of the person driving the vehicle. The second drinking and driving law is the "Operating While Intoxicated" law. (11) Both of the above charges are considered class "D" felonies if the driver had a previous conviction for drunk driving in within five years, or if, while they are operating their vehicle while intoxicated, they cause serious bodily injury to someone. (4) The most important part of the OWI law is the "Implied Consent Law." This law makes it a requirement for all licensed drivers to submit to chemical tests when stopped by a police officer who has probable cause to believe that they may be under the influence of alcohol or some type of drug. (14) If the driver refuses to submit to the chemical tests offered by the officer, the state considers that refusal "prima facie evidence" that the driver is intoxicated. (15) The driver will, in addition to being charged with operating while intoxicated, also be charged with refusing to comply with the "state Implied Consent Law." They will have their license suspended for one year.

Is there too much emphasis placed on drinking and driving? Let's check the facts. Drunk driving in this country causes people to suffer at every level. Most people never realize how large or serious the problem is until they themselves are affected by it. The "Insurance Institute" estimated that 26,000 Americans would die as a result of a drunk driver in 1984, and another 1.5 million people would be injured in some way by a drunk driver. (17) "Allstate® Insurance" estimated that at least twenty-five percent of the insurance premium that you pay goes for damage caused by the drunk driver. (17) Damage done by drinking motorists is often charged to the victim's insurance policy because drunk drivers often will not have auto insurance, or they will leave the scene of the accident. Their fear of an arrest is greater than their sense of moral responsibility. It is not uncommon for a drunk driver to cause several accidents on the same day, going from one "hit and run" accident to another. I have had drunk drivers who were involved in as many as six separate accidents. I remember one hot and humid midnight shift when I investigated an accident involving 16 cars.

When I arrived, I could see cars parked along the east curb by a park. They looked like all of them had been pulled on, twisted out, or smashed into. They all had various types of damage on them ranging from minor scrapes to missing bumpers. I turned the corner to find a newer Chevy Caprice, a two-door station wagon, stopped in front of two marked police cars that had their red lights on.

The driver of the car was sitting behind the wheel staring out through the windshield as if he was mesmerized. He was about 50 years old, kind of heavy-set, round-faced, and clean-shaven. He was unable to stand without help and could not perform the field sobriety tests. He agreed to take a chemical test, and the results indicated that he had enough alcohol in his system to make four men impaired.

While working accident investigation on another day, I saw the saddest situation of my life. At this accident scene, I looked on as this slight, little person was taken from a car. So pretty and peaceful, I thought, as I saw her right profile.

As her face came fully around and exposed to me, I could see that the left side was gone, removed by the impact. She was killed instantly when the car she was in was hit by a truck driven by a drunk driver. He got out of the truck and fell to the ground. I could smell beer on his breath. He was loaded. His blood test was well over 0.4% BAC, and he was charged with operating while intoxicated. He was found guilty on two counts and was sentenced to 20 years in prison. Everyone lost!

I myself almost became the victim of a drunk motorist one day. I was driving down this lonely road going westbound in the middle of the night. I was in a sharp turn in the road when I saw a car coming the other way. He was flying, and I mean going like "demons" were after him. As he got close to me, he started to swerve back and forth, but not as if he was out of control—more like he was playing chicken with me. He was now on my side of the road, coming right at me head-on.

I pulled off the road and had the bumper of my squad up against and touching the guard rail. He pulled back onto his side of the road, still going fast enough to qualify for the Indianapolis 500 race. When I stopped him, he was crying and drunk. His depression was increased by the alcohol even though he was using it to forget his problems. Alcohol and traffic-related fatalities are not always because of the driver's impairment.

Sometimes alcohol is used to give people the courage they need to commit suicide. I was sent to Calumet and the expressway regarding a woman that jumped off onto the expressway. The driver of the truck that hit her was so distraught that the paramedics took him to the hospital where he had a heart attack and died later that week. I found out later that day that this lady had been despondent for some months after losing her son. He died in a car accident in another state, I don't know exactly where. Her sadness was just too much for her to handle. She walked back and forth for hours over the bridge that covered the expressway. The autopsy showed that she had a very high blood alcohol content. People don't need cars and trucks to hurt themselves after drinking too much. One early morning, a young kid almost froze to death because he drank too much and fell asleep in his friend's car. His friends went into a house and left him in the car. When he woke up, he was freezing and trying to get into someone's home to keep from dying from the cold. He was crawling over piles of snow, standing, and falling again, acting as though he was going crazy. He was only wearing a T-shirt and pants. I stopped the car, and he "charged" at me, screaming, "Help me!" He begged me to let him into my car. I let him in the front seat and turned the heat up on high.

Alcohol plays a role in accidents that occur in industry. Although more statistical information is available for traffic accidents, there is enough information to indicate that on-the-job accidents may be a result of alcohol. In 1982, a Maryland study indicated that about 11% of workers who died on the job or in job-related accidents had blood alcohol levels of 0.08% or greater. (18) Another study revealed that alcoholics were "5 times more likely to die from falls than non-alcoholics." (18) I remember an industrial accident where a railroad switchman was coupled between two cars. I was sent to a switching yard for the railroad regarding this accident. The man was kept alive to say goodbye to his family and then died. There were indications that he had been drinking on the job and may have become careless from the alcohol.

Persons on certain addictive medications, such as Valium, for example, are warned not to use alcohol as it may result in a serious additive effect. (20) Sometimes these combined effects give despondent persons the courage to end their lives in other ways, such as the young boy who hung himself in his apartment. The youth left a note written with a very shaky hand which said, "I'm not happy with my life. I can't be happy no matter what I do. My stomach hurts from something I drank yesterday. I thought it would kill me then but it just hurts, I was." He didn't finish it. During the autopsy, they discovered alcohol and drugs in his system in large amounts.

Alcohol abuse causes family deterioration and ultimately divorce in some cases. In fifteen years of handling family fights, I would feel safe to say that alcohol was used by one or both of the arguing parties in over 90% of the incidents. I was talking to the male half of the family fight and as I turned I saw a woman with a gun pointed right at my stomach as she fired a second time. She had a very high amount of alcohol in her system.

Years ago, while walking the beat downtown, I came across the path of a guy who made another error in judgment because of his drinking. I was "breaking in" a new policeman, walking on the midnight shift. We were walking together in the area of Central and Lewis when a car being chased the wrong way screeched to a stop. I walked up to the car, but before I could say anything, a guy pulled up on a motorcycle. "You bastard!" he yelled. He was talking to the driver of the car. This guy on the bike was drinking and had no respect for the law or us officers. Several of his friends arrived and they also were drunk.

Alcohol is a product society would have been better off never discovering.

(1) "Webster's New World Dictionary"

(2) Collier's Encyclopedia #6 1969

(3) Northwestern University's publication "Medical Effects of Alcohol"

(4) "The Whole College Catalog About Drinking: A Guide to Alcohol Abuse and Prevention," 1976

(5) Institute of Police Technology and Management, University of North Florida, "Administering a DWI Program," 1986

(6) State Code 7.1-2-3-7

(7) State Code 35-47-1-2

(8) State Code 35-50-2-10

(9) State Code 7.1-5-1-3

(10) State Code 9-11-2-1

(11) State Code 9-11-2-2

(12) State Code 9-11-2-3

(13) State Code 9-11-2-4

(14) State Code 9-11-4-2

(15) State Code 9-11-4-7

(16) State Code 9-11-4-9

(17) Allstate Insurance pamphlet "The Drunk Driver May Kill You," 5th Special Report to the U.S. Congress on Alcohol and Health

(18) From the Secretary of Health and Human Services, December 1983

(19) "The Whole College Catalog About Drinking: A Guide to Alcohol Abuse Prevention"

(20) Physician's Desk Reference (PDR), 40th edition, 1986

It only stands to reason that a person would be more prone to commit certain crimes while under the influence of alcohol; what I mean is that the first area of the brain affected by alcohol is that which influences judgment and morals. (1) Over the decades, there have been studies showing a correlation between drinking and crime. (2) Another shocking report in 1958 reported that in 2/3 of the murder cases reviewed, there was drinking prior to the crime by either the murderer, the victim, or both. While rape and alcohol correlations are hard to make, because of the under-reported nature of the crime and the overused alibi of intoxication by the offender, studies have found that rapists often drank very heavily before the crime and that their overall consumption of alcohol was two to three times the normal amount. (2) Northwestern Traffic Institute's lesson "Medical Effects of Alcohol." (2) 5th Special Report to the U.S. Congress on Alcohol and Health from the Secretary of Health and Human Services, December 1983.

Chapter 24: Caught Leaving a Liquor Store

It's January 27, 5 p.m., and I'm all "mixed up" as far as my emotions go. I'm trying to figure out a way to attend my college class; I am finishing my B.A. degree in criminal justice. But the chances of that are becoming less and less as the shift moves along. You see, I'm working afternoons, and we have several cases going on and ready to come to a head any minute. My partner and I have a burglary with a loss of over $8,000.00 we are about to make a pick up on. Another team of detectives is trying to pick up a guy they have an "I.D." on for an armed robbery. This guy in the robbery is a "high priority" because he runs with three other robbers, and we think the combined number of armed robberies they are responsible for is over 30 in the county. So as you can imagine, I'm excited, nervous, and somewhat disappointed.

I determined that I was not going to attend class, so I made arrangements to drop off my assignment at school. Well, after dropping my homework off, I returned to checking locations where this robbery suspect may be. I heard several other detective units talking on the radio, and it was apparent that there were four detective units around this guy's house. I, myself, was checking the Far East area around businesses that he and his confederates liked to hit on a regular basis. There are three businesses that this guy and his comrades have hit at least four times each. I did not see any unusual activity around any of them.

I found out that they had hit a restaurant in that east area in the short time I was out of the car at school. I went into an area where they may be going, as they have a habit of going to some places where they feel safe after getting a good score. I checked some of the taverns and nightclubs they went to quite a bit. I met another detective unit on a quiet, dark, dead-end street with our lights off. They were very agitated because they could not find any of them. They told me that they had been looking for hours with no luck. These culprits use the same cars and these detectives could not find the guys or cars anywhere.

As we talked, a car pulled up on my right. "Holy crap," one of my partners said, "that's the car!" Bigger than life, there the car was, and inside we could see through the frosted, dirty windows the face of the driver, who was the object of our search. Our captain said not to try and "take these guys down alone" because they all carry guns and have shot at cops before. With this in mind, we tried to call for a couple of beat cars. Before I could complete the request, they started to pull out of this drive and were leaving. "Let's take them," one of the detectives said. His partner put their car in reverse, backed up squealing tires, and blocked off this car's exit. I threw my car in drive, floored it, and then screeched to a stop, almost touching the driver's door with my bumper. I was so close that when the driver opened the door to get out, he could only open it about an inch. After trying to exit his door and failing, he climbed over another guy in the front seat. He was out the passenger door in a matter of seconds, crawling on his hands and knees.

He got to his feet and began to run for the field located behind the rear of his car. I got out of my car, with my gun in hand, and climbed on top of the hood of my car. I was afraid if I ran around my car I would lose sight of him, and there was no room between the two cars for me to get by. Sometimes I surprise myself, and this was one of those times. I could see by their expressions on their face that both this suspect and I were amazed at the speed I climbed over this car.

I jumped to the ground and began to run at him on an intersecting course. As I got close to him, he looked over at me and threw his hands straight up into the air as if something had pulled them up on a hoist. "Don't shoot. I'll stop," he yelled as he tried to stop on the snow-covered lot without losing his balance.

"On the ground," I yelled to him while pointing my gun with my right hand and holding my badge over my head with the other hand. "Police officers," I yelled to him as I walked up to his sprawled-out form on the ground.

"I know, man, but what's the problem?" he asked.

"You're under arrest for probable cause armed robbery," I told him as I cuffed him.

After cuffing him, I knelt with my knee on his arm with just enough pressure to keep him face down but not so much that it would hurt him. He and I were at the rear of the car, and as I held this guy down, I pointed my gun at the rear window of their car. The other detectives, now out of their car, were also aiming at the car. Before they got out, they gave our location and made a request for backup. I could hear multiple sirens approaching our location. As the patrol units pulled up, they took the guy I had cuffed and placed him in the one squad car. As we took the occupants of the car out, we found two of them were carrying handguns, and another had a sawed-off rifle on the floor by him. We took them all into the station and placed various charges on them.

My regular partner, who was trying to locate the guy he and I were going to pick up later for a burglary, came into the station and said he had found him, and we were ready to go and get him. This suspect lived in town but worked in another city, and that's where he was at. We went to where he worked and waited 15 minutes until he got off work. We could have taken him off the job, but for the extra 15 minutes, it wasn't worth possibly getting him fired or someone hurt. He came out, walked up to his car, and opened the door, which was an old, tan, Ford, two-door. I walked up and showed him my badge. I told him that he was going to have to come with us and that we wanted to talk to him about the burglary. He agreed, as if he was expecting us. Another employee came up as we were talking, obviously concerned over his fellow worker's safety. "You OK, Ted?" he asked. Ted didn't say anything, and this fellow worker then addressed us. "What's going on?" he asked in an aggressive tone.

He was about 6'1", 230 lbs, and was opening his coat to show us that he was in good shape. He had a T-shirt on, and we could see at a glance he was muscular and his stomach flat, as if he was a fighter. My partner showed him his ID and badge and told him everything was okay. He apologized and walked away. I never mind explaining something like that because if more people helped each other, there would be less crime, and it really must have looked strange for two guys in plain clothes to be patting down another guy.

Without getting into a lot of facts about the case, Ted told us who the other people were that were involved in the actual burglary and agreed to give us a written statement. He actually was not involved in the crime but just bought some of the coins from them. We went to his home about 2:00 a.m. and he gave us the items he bought. These coins totaled about $1,200.00 in face value and about $3,000.00 in actual sale value. After returning to the station, inventorying the recovered coins, and completing a daily activity report, I was happy to be on my way home. I was mentally drained; it was a long but great day.

Chapter 25: Not Fan Mail

Dear Officer:

I don't know why you're making such a big deal about this woman; she's probably better off now anyway. I picked her up and used her many times before. She was just a worthless prostitute! She used heroin all the time, and she was only happy when she was high. If you want to compare things, just look at her and me. I have a job and make a good living. I pay taxes, which she did not. I have a wife and children. The only fault you can find with me is that I enjoy sex with cheap whores! Big deal!

You know as well as I do, she would walk all over the street looking to be picked up. She was always wearing those short skirts, black stockings, and low-cut blouses. Hell, half of her breasts were hanging out all the time, and you know it. When someone did pick her up, she set the price, not the customer! Not me! If you really cared about her so much, like you gave the impression of at my trial, why didn't you and the rest of your brothers keep her off the streets? Don't give me any crap either because this woman and others told me how she had to "service" your brothers so she wouldn't go to jail. But I don't care; go ahead and sit in your ivory tower!

As far as her death, you really piss me off because you won't believe it was an accident. She liked being choked and passing out. I just misjudged and held her too long. I don't believe you're pushing this so hard; just think, who other than you, cares about her? Her parents wouldn't even come to my trial. They knew she was a worthless slut! If I die, you bastard, I just hope you can live with yourself, all your bullshit talk about human life, what about me? Please ask the judge. I know he will put a lot of weight on your request. Don't let me die!

Another Victim

Made in the USA
Monee, IL
04 November 2026

67384404R00049